MEAT
GRILLING

MEAT
GRILLING

HAMLYN

First published in 1998
by Hamlyn
an imprint of Reed Consumer Books Limited
Michelin House, 81 Fulham Road, London SW3 6RB
and Auckland, Melbourne, and Singapore.

Copyright © 1998 Reed Consumer Books Limited

ISBN 0 600 59557 9

Printed in Hong Kong

Photographer: Hilary Moore
Home Economists: Lucy Knox & Sarah Lowman

Contents

Meat Grilling

Grilling is one of the healthiest and most delicious ways of cooking meat as well as the oldest. Since prehistoric times, man has enjoyed the wonderful flavors and aromas of meat cooked over an open fire. Crisp, golden, and crunchy on the outside; tender, succulent, and juicy inside, grilled meat takes on a new dimension on hot summer days when it can be cooked outside on a barbecue. It is the ideal food for family meals and impromptu parties, and it can be enjoyed anywhere at any time—in your backyard, at the shore, during the day, or under the stars.

The other good thing about grilling is that it requires only minimum culinary skills and even a novice can be successful. Timing is all-important as it is essential not to let the meat overcook. Just follow the guidelines for success below.

Tips for successful grilling

Get the barbecue hot

If using an outdoor charcoal grill, light it about an hour in advance of when you plan to cook so as to give it plenty of time to heat up. When the flames die down, the coals glow red, and a dull grey dust forms on them, the barbecue is ready and you can start cooking. If using a gas or an electric grill, turn it on about 5 minutes ahead of cooking. The grill must be very hot to sear the outside of the meat and seal in the juices.

Be prepared

When barbecuing, always keep two bowls beside you: one of water in case of flare-ups when you need to extinguish the flames; and one of marinade, oil, melted butter, or a sauce for basting the meat while it cooks.

The right temperature

Make sure that the meat is at room temperature. Remove it from the refrigerator at least 1 hour before grilling. It will cook evenly if the temperature is uniform. Frozen meat should be thoroughly defrosted.

Use good-quality meat

It is important to use best-quality lean meat for grilling. Steaks, lamb and pork chops, chicken, veal, game, sausages, and burgers are all suitable. If possible, the meat should be cut to the same size so that it can cook evenly together.

Prepare the grid

To prevent the meat sticking while it is being grilled, you should rub some fat or brush some oil over the grid of the barbecue before adding the meat. Alternatively, you can arrange the meat on a sheet of oiled kitchen foil or in a special foil container which can be placed directly over the hot coals.

Experiment with marinades

Marinades help to flavor and tenderize the meat. Do not throw away any leftover marinade; use it to baste the meat while it is cooking to keep it moist. Alternatively, you can baste with oil or melted butter.

Use tongs

Do not prick or pierce the meat while it is cooking, or its delicious juices will escape. Use long-handled tongs to turn the meat rather than knives or long-handled forks.

Adding salt

Never add salt to the meat before grilling. Salt tends to draw out the succulent juices and causes the meat to dry out and harden. You can salt the meat just before serving, according to individual taste.

Watch the grill

Always keep an eye on the meat while it is cooking to prevent it burning or becoming overcooked. Too much flame is disastrous and the food could end up a burnt offering of unappetizing charcoal.

Protect yourself

Accidents do happen and it is important to take sensible precautions and protect yourself from flames and heat when grilling. Use oven gloves, long-handled forks, and meat tongs to protect your arms and hands.

Grilling chicken

It is essential to cook chicken thoroughly, even though beef and lamb can be eaten pink. One way to do this is to cook chicken pieces, halved and butterflied poultry bone-side down on the grill. This enables the bone to act as a heat conductor. When the underside is cooked, turn the chicken over and cook the fleshy side until done and the skin is crisp.

Serve immediately

Meat is best served really hot straight from the grill. It cannot be reheated successfully and tends to be tough when it gets cold.

The process of grilling

Grilled meat is cooked by being directly exposed to a fierce source of heat. In order to concentrate the flavors within the meat, intense heat is essential and the cooking process should be very fast. If the grill is not hot enough, the meat will not sear, a protective golden crust will not form, and the juices will run out. Beef, lamb, and game should be seared very quickly on both sides close to the heat, whereas pork, veal, and chicken can be cooked more slowly and further from the heat.

Plan ahead

To save time and enjoy grilled food at its best, it always helps to plan ahead. Here are a few useful tips to help you.

- Prepare the meat in advance and store in the refrigerator until 1 hour before it is required, then allow it to come up to room temperature.
- Make the marinade ahead and marinate the meat for the required time, until needed.
- You can also make flavored butters and sauces in advance and freeze or refrigerate them until required.

Grills, fuel, and equipment

There is a wide range of grills that you can use, whether indoor or outdoor. All barbecue cooking implements need long handles to protect you from the heat and flames.

Built-in cooker grill (broiler)

This may be an overhead grill (broiler) at eye or waist level or within your oven. With these grills, you can adjust the distance between the food and the heat source, as well as controlling the intensity of the heat. When grilling indoors, you should have adequate ventilation as grilling can cause a lot of smoke.

Brazier-type barbecue

This is the most basic type of barbecue, consisting of a shallow bowl or "kettle" in which the charcoal is lit. The air flows over the charcoal while the meat is cooking. These barbecues may have a hood or windshield and sometimes incorporate a rotisserie for spit-roasting meat.

Grill-type barbecue

In this sort of barbecue, air vents allow the air to flow up and through the charcoal while the food is cooking.

Gas barbecue

These barbecues are expensive but ideal for fast grilling as they take only five minutes to heat up, and you have instant heat control, usually with high, medium, and low settings. However, to real outdoor grilling aficionados they smack of cheating and they cannot impart the special, distinctive flavor and aroma of char-grilled food.

Fuel

Charcoal is the normal fuel for outdoor grills, normally in briquet or lump wood form. However, you can also use seasoned, dried hardwood, fruitwood, such as apple, or hardwood chips.

Hickory chips

Aromatic hickory and mesquite chips can be sprinkled on the fire below the meat to add a characteristic smoky flavor. Most of these chips must be soaked in water before use but you can buy "smoke chips" which require no soaking. You could also try sprinkling fresh herbs on the hot coals.

Drip trays

Foil trays are useful for placing beneath the meat while it is cooking to catch the juices and fat. If wished, you can use these to baste the meat.

Kebob skewers

Kebobs make brilliant grills—easily prepared and quickly cooked, they are the perfect fast food for busy cooks. Flat metal skewers tend to be preferable to round ones which can turn over involuntarily while cooking. Always presoak wooden skewers in water for 30 minutes before use.

Other equipment

Always wear oven gloves when handling even long-handled forks and tongs to turn and remove food from the grill. And when cooking outdoors, remember to take out a trash bag for all the trash, paper plates, and leftovers.

Flavoring the meat

You can add flavor to meat with savory butters, marinades, sauces, herbs, and spices.

Flavored butters

Adding a knob of savory butter to meat during or after cooking will enhance its natural flavor. The butter can be prepared in advance and then rolled into a sausage shape, wrapped in kitchen foil or waxed paper, and chilled or frozen until required.

Try adding the following flavorings:

- Minced garlic and herbs
- Chopped anchovy fillets
- Finely chopped onion or scallions
- Tomato paste and spices
- Very finely chopped fresh or dried chilies
- Dijon mustard

Marinades

These are highly flavored liquid mixtures in which the meat can be soaked before grilling. They help to tenderize the meat and to keep it moist while cooking as well as adding flavor. Generally, the longer the meat is marinated, the more flavor it absorbs. It should be turned frequently in the marinade and then drained thoroughly and patted dry with paper towels before grilling. Marinades can be made with the following ingredients:

- Olive, corn, nut, and sesame oils
- Fruit juices
- Plain yogurt
- Ground and whole spices, and fresh ginger root
- Fresh and dried herbs
- Honey, hoisin sauce, soy sauce, and tomato paste
- Finely chopped chilies
- Minced garlic and finely chopped onion

Sauces

A wide range of sauces can be served with grilled meat, many of which can be purchased ready-made.

- Barbecue sauce complements steaks, chops, sausages, and chicken pieces.
- Béarnaise sauce, flavored with tarragon, is the classic accompaniment for steaks.
- Tomato ketchup is the ubiquitous and traditional accompaniment for steaks, burgers, and sausages.
- Horseradish sauce goes well with grilled beef.
- Salsas make a fresh, spicy addition to meat, game, and chicken.
- Yogurt, flavored with chives, mint, lemon, spices, or cucumber, is wonderful with grilled chicken and lamb.

Meat for grilling

There is a wide range of meat, poultry, and game that can be grilled, including the following:

Steak

Always use good-quality thick steaks, such as filet mignon, rib-eye, T-bone, porterhouse, flank, New York strip, or beef tenderloin steaks. There is no need to marinate steaks unless you want to add a specific flavor. If you are in a hurry or prefer a plain grilled steak, just rub it with a cut clove of garlic before grilling, or brush with oil or melted butter. A good sprinkling of freshly ground black pepper adds the finishing touch. Steaks may be served "bleu," rare, medium, or well done (see cooking times in individual recipes and the section on testing when the meat is cooked, page 11). You can also grill a whole beef fillet or triangle tips.

Pork

It is best to use lean good-quality pork that requires minimum cooking—chops, tenderloin (fillet), and spareribs are ideal. Unlike steak, pork should never be served pink and you must make sure that it is thoroughly cooked.

Lamb

The usual cuts for grilling are chops, steaks cut from the boned leg, the fillet, or even the whole leg on the bone. Lamb tastes especially delicious when marinated before cooking. You could try red wine and herbs, or a garlic and yogurt mixture, flavored with mint or spices, as is common in many Middle Eastern dishes. A good way to serve a barbecued leg of lamb is to make small incisions in the flesh before cooking and then insert slivers of garlic and sprigs of rosemary. Lamb may be served pink or well-cooked.

Chicken and poultry

Chicken and duck can both be grilled to a succulent, crisp-skinned perfection. You can use chicken thighs, drumsticks, breasts, or joints. Brush with oil, melted butter, or a marinade before grilling. Chicken must always be well cooked, never pink. If the grill is too hot, there is a danger that the skin can get crisp and burnt before the flesh inside is cooked. To avoid this, use small pieces rather than large ones, do not over-heat the grill, and cook the chicken further away from the heat than you would with steak or lamb.

To test whether the chicken is cooked, use a sharp pointed knife to pierce the thickest part. The juices must run clear.

Burgers

These can be made with ground beef, lamb, or pork. Alternatively, they can be flavored, if you wish, with onion, garlic, herbs, spices, salt and pepper, and the mixture bound with a beaten egg. Serve in buns with melted cheese, lettuce, sliced tomato, and gherkins.

Other meat

Veal, kidneys, liver, and game can also be grilled successfully. Take care when cooking veal as it must be well cooked. Rabbit pieces, and game birds such as small pheasants, partridges, quail, and even venison taste sensational if marinated and then grilled until cooked and crisp.

Kebobs

Steak, lamb or pork fillet, chicken, and turkey can all be cut into cubes, marinated and then threaded on to kebob skewers, as can chicken livers, small sausages, and bacon-wrapped prunes. Vary the flavor with cherry tomatoes, chunks of red onion, bell peppers, zucchini, mushrooms, and bay leaves. Brush frequently with oil or marinade while grilling to prevent them drying out, and turn several times so that the meat cooks evenly.

Testing if meat is cooked

It is difficult to give exact cooking times when grilling meat as people's individual preferences differ, as does the temperature of the grill. The following guidelines should prove helpful. Times given are for 1-inch thick steaks.

"Bleu" (blue)

This is for people who like their steak very rare indeed. The meat is seared very quickly over intense heat so that it is cooked on the outside but still rare to blue when cut open. The steak should offer no resistance when you press it lightly with a finger. Cooking time: approximately 5 minutes.

Rare

When it is sliced, rare meat should still be pink on the inside with the juices running freely. This is suitable for steak, lamb, game, and kidneys. When grilling the meat, turn it over when the blood can be seen on the surface. Again, when pressed, the meat should offer little resistance. Cooking time: approximately 7 minutes.

Medium

When cut, medium-cooked meat should be just slightly light pink inside with the juices set. You can enjoy steak, lamb, kidneys, liver, veal, and duck cooked in this way. Grill the meat in the usual manner until drops of juice appear on the surface, then turn it over and cook the other side. The meat should resist slightly when you press it with a finger. Cooking time: approximately 14 minutes.

Well done

You can cook steak and lamb in this way if that is how you like it, but it is absolutely essential when cooking pork and chicken. Grill the meat until there is no trace of pink inside, the center is beige but still juicy, and it resists when pressed lightly with a fork or finger. Cooking time: approximately 15–16 minutes.

WHOLE CHICKEN ON A SPIT

bunch of mixed herbs, e.g. sage, bay
leaves, thyme, and parsley
I lemon, quartered
3½-pound free-range chicken
½ stick butter, melted
salt and pepper

1 Place the herbs and lemon in the cavity of the chicken and season.
2 Using kitchen string, place the chicken, back downward, with the center of the string beneath its tail end. Cross the string over the tail and loop each end around the opposite leg, pulling the ends away from the chicken to bring the drumsticks over the cavity. Turn the chicken over, take one string up to the thigh and loop it over the wing, then across the neck flap. Repeat on the other side. Knot the string at the center back.
3 Brush the chicken all over with melted butter and season with salt and pepper. Carefully insert the rotisserie spit.
4 Secure the chicken about 8 inches above the coals of a preheated barbecue and cook for 1¼–1½ hours, turning and basting frequently.
5 To check that the chicken is cooked, insert a skewer into the thickest part of the thigh. If the juices run clear it is done.
6 Remove the chicken to a serving dish and carve. Serve with Tomato Relish (see below) or Yellow Bell Pepper Dip (see opposite).

Serves 4
Preparation time: 15 minutes
Cooking time: 1¼–1½ hours

TOMATO RELISH

3 cups skinned and chopped ripe tomatoes
3 cups deseeded and finely chopped
red bell peppers
2 cups finely chopped onions
2 red chilies, deseeded and finely chopped
2 cups red wine vinegar
¾ cup soft brown sugar
4 tablespoons mustard seeds
2 tablespoons celery seeds
I tablespoon paprika
2 teaspoons salt
2 teaspoons pepper

1 Place all the ingredients in a large pan and slowly bring to the boil. Simmer, uncovered, for about 30 minutes, until most of the liquid has evaporated and the relish is of a thick, pulpy consistency. Stir frequently as the relish thickens.
2 Pour into clean, sterilized jars. To sterilize the jars, put the clean jars, open end up, on a cookie sheet and place in a preheated cool oven at 275°F for about 10 minutes, until hot. Seal with vinegar-proof covers when cool.

Makes about 3 pounds
Preparation time: 20 minutes, plus cooling time
Cooking time: 40 minutes

LEMON CHICKEN

4 boneless, skinless chicken breasts

Lemon marinade:
finely grated zest and juice of 1 lemon
3 tablespoons virgin olive oil
1 teaspoon clear honey
1 garlic clove, sliced
parsley sprig

To garnish:
parsley sprigs
lemon slices

1 Mix together the marinade ingredients in a small pitcher. Make 4 diagonal slashes in each chicken breast. Place the chicken in a shallow bowl and pour over the marinade. Cover and leave to marinate for 4 hours in a cool place, turning occasionally.

2 Remove the chicken breasts from the marinade and place each breast on to individual double-thickness pieces of kitchen foil. Turn the edges of the foil in towards the center, spoon over the lemon marinade, and secure tightly.

3 Place each foil parcel on the grill of a preheated barbecue and cook for 10 minutes. Turn the foil parcels over and cook for a further 10 minutes, or until the chicken is tender.

4 Open the parcels and transfer the chicken to 4 warmed serving plates. Spoon over some of the cooking juices and garnish with sprigs of parsley, and lemon slices. Serve with a green salad.

Serves 4
Preparation time: 10 minutes, plus 4 hours marinating time
Cooking time: 20 minutes

YELLOW BELL PEPPER DIP

2 yellow bell peppers
2 tablespoons plain yogurt
1 tablespoon dark soy sauce
1 tablespoon chopped fresh cilantro
(optional)
pepper

1 Put the yellow bell peppers under a preheated broiler for about 10 minutes, turning occasionally until well charred and blistered. Place in a plastic bag until cool, then deseed, and put the flesh in a food processor or blender with the yogurt, and blend until smooth.

2 Pour into a bowl, season with soy sauce and pepper to taste, stir in the chopped cilantro, if using. Cover and chill until required.

Serves 4
Preparation time: 5 minutes, plus cooling time
Cooking time: about 10 minutes

PARMESAN CHICKEN DRUMSTICKS

$^1/_2$ cup fresh white bread crumbs
3 tablespoons finely shredded
Parmesan cheese
I tablespoon all-purpose flour
4 large chicken drumsticks, skinned
I egg, beaten
salt and pepper

I Mix together the bread crumbs and Parmesan cheese. Season the flour with salt and pepper. Coat the chicken drumsticks with the seasoned flour, dip in the beaten egg, then roll in the bread crumb and cheese mixture, pressing it on well with the fingertips. Make sure the drumsticks are thoroughly coated with the mixture, then cover and leave to chill in the refrigerator for 30 minutes.
2 Cook the chicken drumsticks on the oiled grill of a preheated barbecue for 30–40 minutes, turning frequently, until tender and cooked through.
3 Serve the chicken drumsticks with Tomato Relish (see page 12).

Serves 4
Preparation time: 10 minutes, plus chilling
Cooking time: 30–40 minutes

STUFFED CHICKEN BREASTS

3 tablespoons butter
I small onion, finely chopped
$^1/_2$ cup brown rice
I teaspoon turmeric
I bay leaf
3 cloves
2 green cardamom pods
I $^1/_4$ cups water
4 boneless, skinless chicken breasts
salt

I Melt the butter in a pan over a gentle heat. Increase the heat and add the onion and rice and fry until the onion has softened. Add the turmeric, bay leaf, cloves, cardamoms, and salt to taste.
2 Stir in the water and bring to the boil. Lower the heat and simmer gently for about 15 minutes, or until all the water has been absorbed and the rice is tender. Remove the spices from the rice.
3 Put the chicken breasts between 2 sheets of waxed paper and beat with a meat mallet or wooden rolling pin until thin. Place one-quarter of the rice mixture on each chicken breast and roll up. Secure with oiled skewers.
4 Cook on the oiled grill of a preheated barbecue for about 10 minutes each side. Cut into slices to serve, if wished, and serve with a selection of relishes and a salad.

Serves 4
Preparation time: 25 minutes
Cooking time: 20 minutes

CHICKEN SATÉ

A delicacy of Indonesia, this is now a worldwide favorite.
It should be served with skewers of alternating cucumber and onion pieces.

4 large boneless, skinless chicken breasts
⅔ cup soy sauce
2 tablespoons soft dark brown sugar
4 tablespoons molasses
2 large garlic cloves, minced
grated zest of 1 lemon
3 tablespoons lemon juice
1-inch piece fresh ginger root,
peeled and grated

Peanut sauce:
2 cups dry roast peanuts, or salted
peanuts, well rinsed and dried
2 large garlic cloves, halved
3 dried red chilies, deseeded and crumbled
1 onion, coarsely chopped
1 teaspoon salt
4 tablespoons groundnut oil
⅓ cup chicken broth
1 tablespoon soft dark brown sugar
2 tablespoons soy sauce
2 tablespoons lime juice

1 Cut the chicken breasts into 1-inch cubes, then thread on to bamboo skewers. Lay the skewers in a long shallow dish.
2 Mix together the soy sauce, sugar, molasses, garlic, lemon zest and juice, and the ginger, stirring thoroughly, then pour over the chicken skewers. Turn the skewers to coat the meat. Cover and leave for 1 hour in a cool place, turning the skewers 2–3 times.
3 To make the sauce, put the peanuts into a grinder and grind finely, then transfer to a blender. Add the garlic, chilies, onion, salt, and half the oil and blend to a thick paste, adding 1 tablespoon of the chicken broth if necessary to make it blend easily.
4 Heat the remaining oil in a small saucepan, pour in the nut paste and cook gently for 3–4 minutes, stirring constantly. Add the chicken broth and bring to the boil, then lower the heat and simmer gently for 5–10 minutes, until the sauce is very thick and smooth.
5 Remove from the heat and stir in the sugar, soy sauce, and lime juice, mixing well. Keep the peanut sauce warm on the side of the barbecue grill while cooking the chicken.
6 Place the skewers on the preheated greased grill of a barbecue, over hot coals, and cook for 5–6 minutes, turning constantly and basting with the marinade.
7 Serve the hot chicken satés with the peanut sauce.

Serves 6
Preparation time: 30 minutes, plus 1 hour marinating time
Cooking time: 20 minutes

CHICKEN WITH SWEET RAISIN STUFFING

I roasting chicken, weighing 1¾ pounds
2 ounces macaroons
(almond cookies), crushed
I cup coarse bread crumbs
½ cup raisins
I tablespoon chopped basil
I egg, beaten
4 tablespoons olive oil
3 tablespoons honey, melted
I tablespoon lemon juice
I teaspoon ground cinnamon
salt and pepper

1 Rub the chicken inside and out with salt and pepper.
2 Mix together the crushed macaroons (almond cookies), bread crumbs, raisins, chopped basil, beaten egg, and salt and pepper.
3 Stuff the chicken with this mixture and secure the opening with small metal skewers.
4 Rub olive oil all over the stuffed chicken. Fix the chicken securely on a spit, and roast over a preheated barbecue (or in the oven) for 45 minutes.
5 Mix the melted honey with the lemon juice and brush the chicken all over, then sprinkle with the ground cinnamon. Continue roasting on the spit for a further 45 minutes. You can test to check that the chicken is cooked by pricking the thickest part with a fine skewer. If the juices run pink, continue cooking for another 10 minutes.

Serves 6
Preparation time: 15 minutes
Cooking time: 1½–1¾ hours

TANDOORI CHICKEN

4 boneless, skinless chicken breasts
parsley sprigs, to garnish
lime wedges, to serve

Tandoori marinade:
1¼ cups plain yogurt
½-inch piece fresh ginger root,
peeled and finely chopped
I garlic clove, minced
2 teaspoons paprika
I teaspoon chili powder
I tablespoon tomato paste
finely grated zest and juice of ½ lemon
salt and pepper

1 Mix all the marinade ingredients together and season to taste with salt and pepper. Pour into a shallow dish. Prick the chicken breasts all over with a fine skewer and place in the marinade, turning to coat well. Cover and leave to marinate overnight in a cool place, turning the chicken occasionally.
2 Remove the chicken from the marinade and place on the oiled grill of a preheated barbecue. Cook for about 10 minutes on each side, or until the chicken is tender.
3 Garnish with parsley sprigs and serve with lime wedges and a salad.

Serves 4
Preparation time: 10 minutes, plus marinating overnight
Cooking time: 20 minutes

MAPLE CHICKEN WITH ORANGE AND WATERCRESS

4 chicken legs

Marinade:
I cup unsweetened orange juice
I onion, thinly sliced
I garlic clove, minced
freshly ground nutmeg
4 tablespoons maple syrup
salt and pepper

Orange and watercress salad:
4 thin-skinned oranges
I bunch watercress, washed
and shaken dry
I small onion, finely chopped
4 tablespoons olive oil
2 tablespoons chopped chives

1 Pierce the chicken legs at regular intervals with a skewer and put them into a shallow dish. Add the orange juice, onion, garlic, salt, pepper, and nutmeg to taste. Cover and chill for 8 hours.

2 Remove the chicken joints from their marinade, allowing the excess to drip off. Place on a preheated barbecue grill, flesh-side down, and cook for 15 minutes. Turn the chicken joints over, brush with maple syrup and cook for a further 15–20 minutes until tender. Test the chicken by piercing the joints in the thickest part with a fine skewer—if the juices run clear, not pink, the chicken is cooked. Serve the chicken hot with the salad.

3 For the salad, grate the zest and squeeze the juice from 1 orange. Remove all the pith and peel from the remaining 3 oranges and divide into sections. Snip the watercress into sprigs. Put the orange sections and watercress into a serving dish and sprinkle with the onion. Mix the orange juice and zest with the oil, chives, and season with salt and pepper. Spoon the dressing over the salad.

Serves 4
Preparation time: 30 minutes, plus chilling overnight
Cooking time: 30–35 minutes

TURKEY AND CRANBERRY SKEWERS

2 large boneless turkey breasts, skinned
and cut into I-inch dice
I large red bell pepper, deseeded and cut
into I-inch squares
12 button mushrooms
8 bay leaves
6 tablespoons cranberry sauce
2 tablespoons olive oil

1 Thread the turkey, bell pepper, mushrooms, and bay leaves alternately on to 4 oiled kebob skewers.

2 Strain the cranberry sauce into a small heatproof bowl, stir in the oil, and place the bowl over a pan of simmering water. Heat, without boiling, until the sauce is thinner.

3 Brush the cranberry sauce over the kebobs, and cook on the oiled grill of a preheated barbecue for 8–10 minutes, turning frequently and basting with any remaining sauce.

Serves 4
Preparation time: 10 minutes
Cooking time: 8–10 minutes

CINNAMON-SPICED CHICKEN WINGS

8 large chicken wings

Marinade:
1 garlic clove
2-inch piece fresh ginger root, peeled and chopped
juice and finely grated zest of 2 limes
2 tablespoons light soy sauce
2 tablespoons groundnut oil
2 teaspoons ground cinnamon
1 teaspoon ground turmeric
2 tablespoons honey
salt

1 Place all the marinade ingredients in a blender or food processor and blend until very smooth.
2 Place the chicken in a bowl, pour over the marinade, toss, cover and leave to marinate for 1–2 hours.
3 Drain the chicken and cook on a barbecue grill for 4–5 minutes each side, basting with the remaining marinade. Serve with the Yellow Bell Pepper Dip (see page 13).

Serves 4
Preparation time: 10 minutes, plus 1–2 hours marinating time
Cooking time: 8–10 minutes

BUTTERFLIED POUSSIN

2 poussins, cleaned
6 tablespoons oil
1 tablespoon Worcestershire sauce
2 garlic cloves, minced
juice of ½ lemon
1 tablespoon French mustard
salt and pepper

1 Place the poussins on a board, breasts downward. Cut through the backbone, from one end of each poussin to the other. Remove the backbone completely.
2 Open out each poussin and place, skin-side uppermost, on a board. Beat with a meat mallet or rolling pin to flatten each poussin—be careful not to splinter the bones or tear the flesh.
3 Fold the wing tips under the wings, to lie flat. Cut off the feet. Insert 2 skewers, crisscross fashion, to hold the poussins rigid.
4 Mix together the oil, Worcestershire sauce, garlic, lemon juice, mustard, and salt and pepper to taste. Spoon over the poussins in a shallow serving dish. Cover and chill for 4–6 hours, or overnight.
5 Put the poussins, skin-side down, on the rack of a broiler pan. Cook under a preheated moderately hot broiler for 10 minutes. Turn the poussins over and baste with any spare marinade. Cook for a further 10 minutes, until tender.

Serves 2
Preparation time: about 30 minutes, plus 4–6 hours marinating
Cooking time: about 20 minutes

20

POUSSIN STUFFED WITH GOATS' CHEESE

4 poussins
6 ounces soft goats' cheese
1 tablespoon fresh thyme leaves
3 thin slices cured ham, finely chopped
1 lemon, cut into 8 wedges
salt and pepper

Marinade:
1 cup olive oil
finely grated zest of 1 lemon
1 tablespoon chopped fresh basil

1 Rub the poussins inside and out with salt and pepper. Carefully slip your fingers between the skin and flesh of each poussin. Starting at the neck end, gently ease your fingers along the length of the breastbone and down.

2 Mix the cheese with the thyme, ham, and salt and pepper. Ease some of the cheese mixture between the skin and flesh of each poussin. Stuff each body cavity with 2 lemon wedges.

3 Mix the olive oil with the lemon zest, basil, and salt and pepper to taste. Put the poussins into a shallow dish; spoon the marinade over and cover with plastic wrap. Chill for 4 hours.

4 Remove the poussins from their marinade and drain, reserving the marinade.

5 Cook the poussins, breast side down, over a preheated barbecue, for 10 minutes. Turn them over and cook for 15–20 minutes, brushing occasionally with the marinade. Test the poussins by piercing the thickest part with a skewer, the juices should run clear.

Serves 4
Preparation time: 35 minutes, plus 4 hours marinating time
Cooking time: 25–30 minutes

DEVILED CHICKEN

4 chicken drumsticks and 4 chicken wings

Basting sauce:
2 teaspoons chopped rosemary
2 teaspoons chopped parsley
1 teaspoon chopped thyme
2 tablespoons corn oil
2 tablespoons white wine
1 tablespoon soy sauce
2 teaspoons French mustard
few drops of Tabasco sauce
pepper

1 Dry the chicken well, then cut away the tops from the wing joints. Make very light cuts in the chicken flesh so that the basting sauce can penetrate and impart a good flavor to the meat.

2 Blend the ingredients for the basting sauce. Add the chicken and turn around in the sauce until well coated.

3 Place the chicken over a hot barbecue. Cook for about 15 minutes, brushing with the basting sauce several times during cooking.

4 Serve topped with the remaining sauce.

Serves 4
Preparation time: 10 minutes
Cooking time: 15 minutes

BARBECUED DUCK BREASTS

4 duck breast fillets, about 6 ounces each
I quantity orange marinade (see below)
chervil sprigs, to garnish (optional)

I Score the skin of the duck breasts, place them in a shallow dish, and pour over the marinade. Cover and leave to marinate in a cool place for at least 4 hours.

2 Drain the duck breasts and reserve the marinade. Cook under a preheated broiler for about 2 minutes on each side to extract most of the fat and to avoid any flare-up on the barbecue.

3 Place the duck breasts on the oiled grill of a preheated barbecue and cook for 2–6 minutes on each side, according to taste, basting frequently with the reserved marinade.

4 Garnish the duck breasts with chervil sprigs and serve with a colorful mixed salad.

Serves 4
Preparation time: 10 minutes, plus marinating time
Cooking time: 8–16 minutes

ORANGE MARINADE

finely grated zest and juice of I orange
I tablespoon dark soy sauce
3 teaspoons clear honey
½-inch piece fresh ginger root,
peeled and finely chopped
salt and pepper

Mix the marinade ingredients together in a small pitcher.

Serves 4
Preparation time: 5 minutes

SPIT-ROASTED GOOSE

1 goose, weighing about 10 pounds
1½ cups finely chopped button mushrooms
2 garlic cloves, minced
14–15 anchovy fillets, finely chopped
2 sticks butter, softened
3 tablespoons chopped parsley
1 goose liver, finely chopped
salt and pepper

1 Rub the goose inside and out with salt and pepper. Prick the skin at regular intervals with a fine skewer.
2 Mix the mushrooms with the garlic, anchovy fillets, softened butter, parsley, goose liver, and salt and pepper to taste. Stuff the goose with the flavored butter, then sew up the opening with fine kitchen string.
3 Fix the goose securely on the spit and cook over a preheated barbecue for 2 hours. Test to see if the bird is sufficiently cooked; if not, continue cooking for a further 20–30 minutes.
4 Carve the goose into fairly large slices to serve.

Serves 6
Preparation time: 25 minutes
Cooking time: 2–2½ hours

VENISON MARINATED IN BEER

4 lean venison cutlets
⅔ cup dark beer
4 tablespoons olive oil
1 garlic clove, minced
2 dried bay leaves, crumbled
1 teaspoon soft light brown sugar
pepper

1 Trim any visible fat from the venison cutlets and place them in a single layer in a shallow dish. Pour over the beer and olive oil. Add the garlic and bay leaves, sugar, and pepper, but do not add salt.
2 Cover the dish and place in the refrigerator to marinate for at least 4 hours, or overnight.
3 Lift the venison cutlets out of the marinade, reserving the liquid. Place the cutlets on a hot barbecue and cook them for 10–12 minutes, turning once. They should be browned on the outside but slightly pink inside. Spoon over the marinade while cooking to prevent the meat drying out. Serve hot with baked potatoes and a crisp salad.

Serves 4
Preparation time: 10 minutes, plus 4 hours marinating time
Cooking time: 10–12 minutes

SPICED YOGURT RABBIT

2 pounds rabbit pieces
5 tablespoons white wine vinegar
1¼ cups plain yogurt
1 onion, chopped
1 garlic clove, minced
3-inch piece fresh ginger root, peeled and grated
finely grated zest and juice of ½ lemon
1 tablespoon garam masala
½ teaspoon chili powder
½ teaspoon turmeric

To garnish:
cilantro leaves
lemon wedges

1 Wash and dry the rabbit pieces. With a sharp knife, slash the flesh at ½-inch intervals.

2 Place the vinegar and yogurt in a food processor. Add the onion, garlic, and ginger and process until smooth. Stir in the lemon zest and juice, garam masala, chili powder, and turmeric.

3 Place the rabbit pieces in a bowl and pour over the yogurt mixture, coating the pieces evenly. Cover the bowl and chill in the refrigerator for 1–2 days, turning the rabbit occasionally.

4 Lift the rabbit pieces from the marinade, shaking off any excess. Place them on a hot barbecue, or under a preheated hot broiler and cook for 10–15 minutes, turning occasionally, until the juices run clear when the joints are pierced with a fine skewer.

5 Serve garnished with cilantro leaves and lemon wedges.

Serves 6
Preparation time: 15 minutes, plus 1–2 days marinating time
Cooking time: 10–15 minutes

QUAIL WITH JALAPEÑO JELLY GLAZE

8 quails
vegetable oil
½ cup jalapeño jelly, mild or hot
3 tablespoons white wine vinegar

1 Cut down the back of each quail, through the bones, and open the bird out flat. Press gently on the breastbone to break it. Thread the birds on to skewers, crosswise.

2 Brush the quails with oil, then put them, skin-side up, on a greased grill, 6 inches above medium coals. Cook for 20–30 minutes, turning occasionally and brushing with more oil as needed.

3 Meanwhile, put the jelly and vinegar in a small saucepan and place on the grill. Heat, stirring, until the jelly has melted. Baste the quails with the jelly glaze during the last 2–3 minutes of cooking, turning the birds so they are glazed all over. Serve hot.

Serves 4
Preparation time: 15 minutes
Cooking time: 20–30 minutes

LAMB WITH CRANBERRIES AND HONEY

4 lean lamb chops or leg steaks
⅔ cup cranberry juice
1 cup fresh or frozen cranberries
3 tablespoons clear honey
mint sprigs, to garnish

1 Trim any visible fat from the lamb and place in a large dish. Pour over the cranberry juice. Cover and leave to marinate for at least 4 hours or overnight. Drain the meat, reserving the marinade.
2 Place the lamb over a hot barbecue, or under a preheated hot broiler, and cook for 7–10 minutes, or until the lamb is cooked to your liking, turning once.
3 Meanwhile, place the marinade in a saucepan with the cranberries and boil rapidly for 5 minutes, or until the cranberries are soft. Add the honey, and stir until it has melted.
4 Serve the lamb with the cranberry sauce spooned over the top.
5 Garnish with sprigs of mint.

Serves 4
Preparation time: 10 minutes, plus marinating time
Cooking time: 7–10 minutes

CRISPY-COATED LAMB WITH ORANGE SAUCE

8 loin lamb chops
I egg white, lightly beaten
3 tablespoons whole wheat bread crumbs
2 tablespoons old-fashioned oats
finely grated zest and juice
of I small orange
⅔ cup plain fromage frais
salt and pepper

To garnish:
orange slices, twisted
chervil sprigs

1 Trim as much fat from the lamb as possible, and brush all over with egg white. In a bowl, mix together the bread crumbs and oats, and season with salt and pepper. Cover the lamb with the crumbs, pressing them all over the chops. Wrap the ends of the bones in foil.

2 Place the lamb over a moderately hot barbecue and cook, turning once, for 8–10 minutes.

3 To make the sauce, combine the orange zest and juice with the fromage frais. When the lamb is ready, serve hot with the sauce spooned over the top. Garnish with orange slices and chervil.

Serves 4
Preparation time: 15 minutes
Cooking time: 8–10 minutes

SPICED LAMB KEBOBS

1½ pounds lamb fillet
2 tablespoons lemon juice
⅔ cup olive oil
2 teaspoons crushed coriander seeds
2 garlic cloves, minced
2 teaspoons ground turmeric
I teaspoon ground ginger
2 teaspoons ground cumin
2 bay leaves, crumbled
2 limes, cut into thin wedges
salt and pepper

1 Trim off any fat from the lamb and cut it into 1-inch dice.

2 Put the lamb into a shallow dish. Mix the lemon juice with the olive oil, crushed coriander seeds, garlic, turmeric, ginger, cumin, crumbled bay leaves, and salt and pepper to taste. Pour this marinade over the meat and stir well.

3 Cover the meat and chill for 12 hours, turning once or twice in the marinade.

4 Remove the meat and drain, reserving the marinade. Thread the meat on to 4 kebob skewers, threading wedges of lime in between some of the cubes. Brush each kebob with some of the marinade.

5 Cook the kebobs on the greased grill of a preheated barbecue (or under an overhead broiler) for 5–8 minutes, until the meat is cooked.

6 Serve the kebobs with hot pita bread.

Serves 4
Preparation time: 20–25 minutes, plus 12 hours marinating time
Cooking time: 5–8 minutes

SPIT-ROASTED LAMB

In this recipe, cook the leg of lamb on a rotating spit over a barbecue—the first slices should be ready to cut and serve within 35–45 minutes, and the meat will continue to cook while the first slices are being enjoyed. This recipe really does need to be spit-roasted, but you can use an oven spit rather than one attached to a barbecue.

1 leg of lamb, weighing 4³⁄₄ pounds

Marinade:
²⁄₃ cup olive oil
1 tablespoon chopped marjoram
2 tablespoons chopped mint
¹⁄₂ teaspoon ground cinnamon
¹⁄₂ teaspoon ground cloves
2 garlic cloves, minced
2 tablespoons rosewater
(for sprinkling during cooking)
salt and pepper

1 With a small knife, make several deep widthwise cuts at regular intervals in the leg of lamb. Put the lamb into a shallow dish.

2 Mix the marinade ingredients together and spoon evenly over the lamb. Cover the lamb and chill for at least 6 hours, turning it from time to time.

3 Remove the lamb from its marinade and drain, reserving the marinade. Fix the lamb securely on to the spit and brush all over with a little of the marinade.

4 Spit-roast over the preheated barbecue for about 35–45 minutes, until the lamb is sufficiently cooked to carve off the outer slices. Leave the rest of the lamb on the spit and carve off slices as they are ready.

5 Serve with warm pita bread and a cucumber and yogurt salad.

Serves 6–8
Preparation time: 10 minutes, plus 6 hours marinating time
Cooking time: 40–50 minutes for the first slices

Note: Rosewater is used in North Africa as a flavoring for lamb, poultry, and sweet dishes. It can be bought at some gourmet food stores or can be made at home. To make rosewater, put 8 ounces unblemished red rose petals in a pan with 2 cups water. Simmer steadily for about 30 minutes, until all the water has been drawn out of the petals and they have become limp. Strain the rose-colored liquid into a clean pan, add ¹⁄₄ cup sugar and stir until dissolved. Simmer for 5 minutes, then cool. Store in a sealed container in the refrigerator for up to 2 weeks.

LAMB KEBOBS WITH YOGURT MARINADE

2 pounds boned leg of lamb,
cut into ¾-inch dice
1 small bunch cilantro leaves, coarsely
chopped
lime or lemon wedges, to serve

Yogurt marinade:
2 cups plain yogurt
3 tablespoons olive oil
2 tablespoons fresh lime juice
1 small onion, shredded
1 teaspoon ground cloves
1 teaspoon cumin seeds, crushed
¼ teaspoon ground cardamom
2 garlic cloves, minced
1 teaspoon ground cinnamon
1 teaspoon salt
1 teaspoon freshly ground white pepper

1 Thread the lamb on to 4 long skewers and place them in a shallow dish or roasting pan.

2 Mix together the ingredients for the marinade and pour over the lamb. Turn the skewers 2–3 times, then cover and leave in a cool place for at least 12 hours, or chill in the refrigerator for 24 hours.

3 Remove the skewers from the marinade, gently shaking off any excess liquid, then cook on a preheated greased barbecue grill, over hot coals, for 10 minutes for rare meat, or 20 minutes for well done. Turn once halfway through the cooking time, and baste with the remaining marinade.

4 Cover a serving dish with a layer of chopped cilantro leaves, then push the meat off the skewers on top of the cilantro. Serve with the lime or lemon wedges, crusty bread and the remaining marinade.

Serves 4

Preparation time: 15 minutes, plus 12 hours marinating time
Cooking time: 10–20 minutes

LAMB AND FETA KEBOBS

2 pounds lean lamb, cut into 1½-inch dice
6 tablespoons olive oil
4 tablespoons lemon juice
2 large garlic cloves, minced
1 tablespoon chopped oregano
1 tablespoon chopped thyme
1 tablespoon chopped marjoram
salt and pepper
4 ounces feta cheese, crumbled, to serve

1 Trim any fat from the lamb and put it in a shallow dish. Mix the olive oil with the lemon juice, garlic, chopped herbs, and salt and pepper to taste. Spoon this marinade evenly over the lamb. Cover the dish and chill for at least 4 hours.
2 Remove the lamb and drain, reserving the marinade. Thread the lamb on to 4 kebob skewers and brush with some of the marinade. Cook on the greased grill of a preheated barbecue (or under an overhead broiler) for about 5 minutes on each side.
3 Sprinkle the kebobs with the crumbled feta cheese. Serve immediately with pita bread and a vegetable dish.

Serves 4
Preparation time: 25 minutes, plus 4 hours marinating time
Cooking time: about 10 minutes

LAMB CHOPS IN RED WINE AND MINT

8 lamb chops, about 1 inch thick
¾ cup red wine
2 tablespoons olive oil
6 tablespoons finely chopped mint
salt and pepper

To garnish:
mint or parsley sprigs
tomato wedges

1 Put the lamb chops in a shallow dish. Mix together the wine, oil, and chopped mint, and pour over the meat. Cover and leave to marinate in a cool place for 1 hour, turning halfway through.
2 Remove the lamb from the marinade and cook on a preheated greased barbecue grill, over hot coals, for 7–10 minutes on each side, according to whether you like your lamb rare or well done. Baste with any leftover marinade before turning.
3 Sprinkle with salt and pepper and serve very hot, garnished with the mint or parsley and tomato wedges. If liked, make a small bowl of yogurt marinade (see page 30) to serve as an accompanying dip.

Serves 4
Preparation time: 5 minutes, plus 1 hour marinating time
Cooking time: 15–20 minutes

MARINATED LEG OF LAMB WITH CREAM SAUCE

The lamb can be spit-roasted in the oven, but it will not have the delicious, golden charred skin that it gets on the grill. Preheat the oven to 375°F, and remove cooked slices as and when they are ready.

1 leg of lamb, weighing 4¾ pounds
1¼ cups dry white wine
1 onion, thinly sliced
handful of celery leaves, coarsely chopped
2 teaspoons juniper berries, crushed
6 tablespoons olive oil
1 cup heavy cream
salt and pepper

1 With a sharp knife, make several deep widthwise incisions in the leg of lamb at regular intervals. Put the lamb into a shallow dish.

2 Mix the white wine with the onion, celery leaves, juniper berries, and salt and pepper to taste, then pour over the lamb. Cover and chill for at least 6 hours, turning the lamb in the marinade from time to time.

3 Remove the lamb from its marinade and drain, reserving the marinade. Fix the lamb securely on to the spit and brush all over with olive oil. Spit-roast over the preheated barbecue for 35–45 minutes, until the lamb is sufficiently tender to carve off the outer slices. If possible, catch the meat juices as the joint cooks.

4 While the lamb is cooking, make the sauce. Put the marinade into a pan and cook rapidly until reduced by half. Stir in any meat juices and the cream. Heat through gently and serve.

5 Keep the sauce warm on the side of the barbecue while the lamb continues to cook. Carve off slices as they are ready.

Serves 6–8
Preparation time: 15 minutes, plus 6 hours marinating time
Cooking time: 35–45 minutes for the first slices

MUSTARD AND HERB GLAZED LEG OF LAMB

I leg of lamb, weighing 5–6 pounds, boned
2–3 garlic cloves, cut into thin slivers
¹/₃ cup Dijon-style mustard
2 tablespoons olive oil
3 tablespoons chopped mint
I tablespoon chopped rosemary
pepper

I Trim as much fat as possible from the lamb. Cut open (butterfly) the leg to make it lie flat. Make incisions all over the meat and insert the garlic slivers.

2 Combine the mustard, oil, herbs, and lots of freshly ground black pepper in a mixing bowl that is large enough to take the lamb comfortably. Stir the ingredients together, then add the lamb and turn to coat with the mustard paste. Rub the paste all over the meat until it is completely coated. Cover and marinate at cool room temperature, or in the refrigerator, for at least 2 hours. (If the lamb has been marinated in the refrigerator, let it return to room temperature before cooking.)

3 Grill the lamb over medium coals for 20–30 minutes on each side. This will produce rare to medium-rare meat; if you prefer lamb well cooked, add 10 minutes more cooking on each side.

4 To serve the lamb, carve it into thin slices across the grain.

Serves 6–8
Preparation time: 15 minutes, plus 2 hours marinating time
Cooking time: 40 minutes–1 hour

LAMB MEATBALLS WITH APRICOT SAUCE

3 cups ground lean lamb
finely grated zest of 1 orange
1 large garlic clove, minced
1 teaspoon apple pie spice
1 small red bell pepper, deseeded and very
finely chopped
2 tablespoons raisins, chopped
2 egg yolks
salt and pepper

Marinade:
5 tablespoons orange juice
6 tablespoons olive oil
3 tablespoons red wine

Apricot sauce:
1 small onion, finely chopped
2 tablespoons olive oil
2 cups fresh or drained
apricots, chopped
1 tablespoon chopped mint
⅔ cup dry white wine
2 teaspoons clear honey

1 Mix the ground lamb with the orange zest, garlic, apple pie spice, red bell pepper, raisins, and salt and pepper to taste. Beat in the egg yolks.

2 Divide the mixture into 20 equal portions and shape each one into a ball. Put in a shallow dish.

3 Mix the marinade ingredients together and spoon over the meatballs. Marinate in the refrigerator, covered, for 4–6 hours, turning them once or twice.

4 To make the apricot sauce, fry the onion gently in the olive oil for 2 minutes. Add the remaining ingredients and simmer gently for 10 minutes.

5 Remove the meatballs from their marinade and drain, reserving the marinade. Take 4 kebob skewers and carefully thread 5 meatballs on to each skewer. Brush evenly all over with the marinade.

6 Cook the meatballs on the greased grill of a preheated barbecue (or under the broiler) for 8–10 minutes, turning them once and brushing with the remaining marinade. Serve the cooked meatballs with the hot sauce.

Serves 4
Preparation time: 30 minutes, plus chilling
Cooking time: 20–22 minutes

SPICED MEAT KOFTAS WITH MINT

2 cups ground lean lamb
I onion, shredded or minced
2 garlic cloves, minced
2 small red chilies, deseeded and finely chopped
3 tablespoons chopped mint
finely grated zest and juice of I small lime
whole wheat flour, for shaping
soya or corn oil, for brushing
salt and pepper
plain yogurt, to serve

To garnish:
lime wedges
mint leaves

I Mix together the lamb, onion, garlic, chilies, mint, lime zest, and juice. Season with salt and pepper.
2 Using lightly floured hands, shape the mixture into 8 small sausage shapes. Thread them on to 4 skewers.
3 Place the koftas over a hot barbecue, or under a preheated moderately hot broiler, and cook for about 10 minutes, turning occasionally, until they are evenly cooked. Brush them with oil while cooking, if necessary, to prevent them drying out.
4 Serve the koftas hot with plain yogurt to spoon over them. Garnish with lime wedges and mint leaves.

Serves 4
Preparation time: 10 minutes
Cooking time: 10 minutes

SPICED LAMB CHOPS

8 lamb chops, fresh or frozen
cherry tomato halves

Marinade:
2 garlic cloves
I teaspoon chopped mint
I teaspoon allspice
$^1\!/_2$ teaspoon ground cinnamon
2 tablespoons oil
2 tablespoons white wine vinegar
2 teaspoons brown sugar
salt and pepper

To garnish:
watercress
mint sprigs

I Defrost the chops if they have been frozen and dry well with paper towels. Peel and mince the garlic. Mix all the ingredients together for the marinade and pour into a long shallow dish. Add the chops and leave to marinate for 1 hour, turning them over after 30 minutes.
2 Lift the meat out of the marinade and hold over the container for a minute so any excess liquid drips off the meat.
3 Grill the chops over hot coals or under a preheated broiler for about 4–5 minutes each side. Add the tomatoes to the grill for the last 2–3 minutes of the cooking time.
4 Arrange the chops and tomatoes on a heated dish, and garnish with the watercress and mint.

Serves 4
Preparation time: 5 minutes, plus 1 hour marinating time
Cooking time: 8–10 minutes

PORK, HAM, AND SAGE ROLLS

¹/₃ cup golden raisins
4 tablespoons Marsala
4 long thin pork steaks (cut from the tenderloin), about 3 ounces each
4 thick slices Parma ham
I tablespoon chopped sage
16 cubes white bread, about I inch square
4 tablespoons olive oil
8 thin slices bacon, rind removed and halved crosswise
salt and pepper

I Mix the golden raisins with the Marsala. Cover and let stand for 1 hour.

2 Cut each pork steak into 4 long strips, then cut the slices of ham into strips roughly the same size.

3 Lay a strip of ham on top of each strip of pork. Sprinkle each strip with some chopped sage, a few of the soaked golden raisins, and salt and pepper to taste. Roll each strip up neatly, so that you have 16 sausage shapes.

4 Brush each cube of bread with a little olive oil, then roll in half a bacon slice.

5 Thread 4 pork and ham rolls and 4 bread and bacon rolls alternately on to each of 4 kebob skewers. Brush the skewers with olive oil.

6 Cook on the greased grill of a preheated barbecue (or under an overhead broiler) for 3–4 minutes on each side. Serve hot with a green salad.

Serves 4
Preparation time: 30 minutes, plus standing time
Cooking time: 7–8 minutes

ORANGE BARBECUED PORK

4 pork chops

Marinade:
I garlic clove
2 teaspoons finely grated orange zest
⅔ cup orange juice
I teaspoon grated ginger root
2 tablespoons sweet sherry
2 tablespoons olive oil

I Cut away any surplus fat from the pork chops. Peel and finely chop the garlic clove and put into a dish with the rest of the marinade ingredients. Put the meat into this mixture and leave for 15 minutes.

2 Remove the pork from the marinade and cook over a preheated hot barbecue for about 20 minutes, turning it several times and brushing with the marinade.

3 Serve with a crisp green salad to which you can add sections of fresh orange, if wished, to enhance the orange flavor.

Serves 4

Preparation time: 5 minutes, plus 15 minutes marinating time
Cooking time: 20 minutes

PASANDA TIKKA

2 cups lean pork, cut into I-inch cubes
3–4 tablespoons plain yogurt
½ teaspoon salt
2 teaspoons mild or hot curry paste
¾ stick butter, melted

To garnish:
2 onions, cut in rings
I lemon, sliced

I Thoroughly prick the meat all over with a fork and place in a large shallow dish. In a bowl, mix the yogurt, salt, and curry paste, and pour over the meat. Cover and marinate for 6 hours.

2 Drain and arrange the meat on 6 small, oiled skewers. Place on a preheated barbecue over medium-hot coals and cook for about 15–20 minutes. Turn and brush occasionally with melted butter.

3 Serve garnished with onion rings and sliced lemon.

Serves 3–4

Preparation time: 5 minutes, plus 6 hours marinating time
Cooking time: 15–20 minutes

STUFFED PORK FILLET

½ cup ground almonds
4 large oranges
2 tablespoons clear honey
4 tablespoons olive oil
2 tablespoons chopped oregano
1 pound pork fillet, trimmed
4 garlic cloves, thinly sliced
1 tablespoon butter, diced
salt and pepper

1 Spread the ground almonds on a cookie sheet. Cook in a preheated oven at 350°F for 10 minutes, until golden. Remove from the oven, let cool, then place in a small bowl.

2 Finely grate the zest from 2 of the oranges and add to the almonds. Add the honey to make a paste, then season to taste. Peel the oranges, divide into sections, and set aside.

3 To make the marinade, squeeze the juice from the 2 remaining oranges into a pitcher. Stir in the olive oil and oregano.

4 Slice each pork fillet lengthwise, almost but not all the way through, and open out like a book. Divide the almond mixture between the fillets. Drain the orange sections, adding any juice to the marinade, and divide them and the garlic slivers between the pork fillets, arranging them on top of the almond mixture.

5 Bring the edges of the meat together and tie the fillets with kitchen string at 1-inch intervals. Place in a shallow dish and pour over the marinade, turning to coat. Cover and refrigerate for 8 hours, or overnight.

6 Let the meat return to room temperature for about 1 hour, then remove from the marinade. Season with salt and pepper and cook on an oiled grill of a preheated barbecue over hot coals for 40–45 minutes, basting frequently with some of the marinade.

7 Transfer the meat to a platter, cover with kitchen foil and leave to rest while you prepare the sauce. Tip the remaining marinade into a small pan and boil rapidly until reduced by half. Slowly beat in the butter.

8 Remove the kitchen string from the pork, slice the meat, and serve with the sauce.

Serves 4
Preparation time: 30 minutes, plus 8 hours marinating time (or overnight)
Cooking time: 40–45 minutes

BARBECUED PORK WITH MUSTARD DRESSING

6 boneless pork loin chops
3 tablespoons whole-grain mustard
4 tablespoons plain yogurt
pepper
lemon wedges, to serve

1 Trim any excess fat from the pork. Mix together the mustard, yogurt, and a little pepper. Spread a thin layer over each chop.
2 Cook the chops over a preheated moderately hot barbecue for about 4 minutes on each side, spreading the second side with the mustard dressing when you turn the chops over.
3 Serve the chops with lemon wedges and a green salad.

Serves 6
Preparation time: 5 minutes
Cooking time: 8 minutes

PORK KEBOBS WITH PRUNES AND CHESTNUTS

1 pound lean pork, trimmed
24 pitted prunes
4 tablespoons Cognac
4 tablespoons olive oil
2 rosemary sprigs, leaves stripped from the stalks, then chopped
24 chestnuts, roasted, dried, or vacuum-packed
salt and pepper

1 Cut the pork into ¾-inch pieces. Place in a bowl with the prunes. Mix the Cognac, olive oil, and rosemary together and pour over the meat. Toss to coat, then cover and marinate overnight in the refrigerator. If using dried chestnuts, soak them in cold water overnight, then drain and treat as fresh.
2 Place the chestnuts in a small saucepan, cover with cold water and bring to the boil. Lower the heat and simmer gently for 15–20 minutes, until tender. Drain, rinse in cold water, and drain again.
3 Using a slotted spoon, remove the meat and prunes from the marinade. Thread on to skewers, alternating with the chestnuts (if the chestnuts are too soft to skewer, stuff one into each prune). Pour the marinade into a small pitcher.
4 Cook the skewers on an oiled barbecue grill over hot coals for about 10–12 minutes, turning them frequently and basting with the marinade. Season with salt and pepper and serve.

Serves 4
Preparation time: 15–25 minutes, plus 12 hours marinating time
Cooking time: 10–12 minutes

BARBECUED PORK SPARERIBS

There is not very much meat on ribs, and, if they are to be eaten as a main course, you need to allow about 1 pound per person. If the grill on the barbecue is widely spaced, leave the ribs in one piece, remembering that they will take longer to cook. Otherwise, separate the ribs, trimming off any jagged edges.

4 pounds pork spareribs
4 tablespoons clear honey

To baste:
6 tablespoons soy sauce
4 tablespoons vegetable oil
3 garlic cloves, peeled and minced
1 small piece fresh ginger root,
or ¼ teaspoon ground ginger
grated zest of 1 lemon
few drops of Tabasco sauce
½ teaspoon ground cinnamon
salt and pepper

1 For the baste, mix the soy sauce with the oil. Add the garlic and ginger, peeled and pressed through a garlic mincer if fresh, the lemon zest, Tabasco, cinnamon, and salt and pepper to taste.

2 Place the ribs on a preheated greased barbecue grill, over hot coals, bone-side downward, and brush with the basting mixture. Cook for about 10 minutes. Turn the ribs over, baste again and cook for a further 15 minutes.

3 Turn the ribs once again and brush with the basting mixture and honey. Cook for another 10–15 minutes.

Serves 4
Preparation time: 5–10 minutes
Cooking time: 35–40 minutes (for separated ribs)

PORK CHOPS WITH GINGERED APPLE AND ROSEMARY SAUCE

Pork and apple sauce are traditional partners. Here is a subtle enhancement, perfumed with
fragrant ginger and rosemary. Grilled parsnips add a touch of sweetness.

4 apples, peeled
leaves from 1 sprig of rosemary,
finely chopped
2 tablespoons clear honey
½ tablespoon grated fresh ginger root
2 tablespoons water
4 pork center-cut chops,
about 10–12 ounces each
1 garlic clove, minced
3 tablespoons olive oil
1 tablespoon sherry vinegar
1 pound young parsnips
2 tablespoons melted butter
salt and pepper

1 Slice each apple into 8 wedges and place in a saucepan with the rosemary, honey, ginger, and measured water. Cover and bring to the boil, then lower the heat and simmer for 10–12 minutes, until the apples are tender. Leave the apple wedges whole or purée in a blender or food processor until smooth.

2 Place the chops in a single layer in a shallow dish. Mix the garlic, olive oil, and vinegar in a pitcher, pour over the pork and turn to coat. Cover and leave to marinate for 1–2 hours.

3 Peel the parsnips and cut them in half lengthwise. Brush them with the melted butter and sprinkle with sea salt. Cook on an oiled barbecue grill over hot coals for 20–25 minutes, turning occasionally.

4 When the parsnips have been cooking for about 10 minutes, drain the chops, reserving the marinade, and add them to the barbecue grill. Cook for 6–7 minutes each side, basting frequently with the marinade.

5 Serve with the grilled parsnips and the gingered apple and rosemary sauce. Grilled asparagus also makes a delicious accompaniment.

Serves 4
Preparation time: 20 minutes, plus 1–2 hours marinating time
Cooking time: 20–25 minutes

PORK AND TANGERINE SKEWERS WITH PEANUT DIP

1 pound lean pork
6 tangerines or 4 small peaches,
pits removed
8 pearl onions, trimmed
8 bay leaves
4 tablespoons smooth peanut butter
2 tablespoons mayonnaise
2 teaspoons lemon juice
1 teaspoon Dijon mustard
olive oil or soya oil
salt and pepper

1 Trim any visible fat from the meat and cut it into 1-inch cubes. Place the pork in a bowl and squeeze the juice from 1 tangerine over the top. If using peaches instead of tangerines, squeeze 3 tablespoons of orange juice over the pork pieces. Toss the pork in the juice and leave it to marinate for at least 1 hour. Lift the pork out of the marinade, retaining the liquid.

2 Cut the remaining tangerines or 4 small peaches into 1-inch pieces. Thread them on to 4 skewers with the pork, whole pearl onions, and bay leaves.

3 Mix together the peanut butter, mayonnaise, lemon juice, mustard, and a little pepper. Place the dip in a serving bowl and garnish with parsley.

4 Sprinkle the skewers with salt and pepper. Place them over a preheated hot barbecue and cook, turning frequently, for about 10–12 minutes. Brush with the marinade and a little oil while they are cooking to prevent the pork drying out.

5 Serve hot with the peanut dip, accompanied by a green salad.

Serves 4
Preparation time: 20 minutes, plus 1 hour marinating time
Cooking time: 10–12 minutes

SWEDISH MEAT CAKES

3 slices white bread, crusts removed
⅔ cup soda water
I cup each ground veal and pork
⅓ cup chopped ham
I teaspoon juniper berries, crushed
2 egg yolks
oil, for brushing
salt and pepper

To serve:
4 large slices rye bread,
spread with sweet butter
I onion, cut into thin rings
2 tablespoons capers
⅔ cup sour cream

1 Break the bread into pieces and put into a shallow dish with the soda water. Let stand for 20 minutes.

2 Mix the ground and chopped meats with the juniper berries, egg yolks, and salt and pepper. Add the bread. Beat the mixture until smooth, then form into 4 meat cakes. Chill for 30 minutes.

3 Brush the meat cakes with oil, then place on a preheated barbecue grill and cook for 4 minutes. Turn the meat cakes over, brush with a little extra oil and cook for a further 4 minutes.

4 Place a slice of rye bread on each serving plate and put a hot meat cake on top. Garnish with a few onion rings, and capers. Add a swirl of sour cream to each plate.

Serves 4

Preparation time: 30 minutes, plus standing and chilling time
Cooking time: 8 minutes

VEAL AND PRUNE KEBOBS

12 large pitted prunes
about ⅔ cup dry white wine
I pound lean veal, in one piece
3 slices ham
3 tablespoons clear honey
3 tablespoons white wine vinegar
oil
salt and pepper

1 Place the prunes in a shallow dish and add sufficient white wine to cover. Let stand overnight, or until plumped up.

2 Cut the veal into 1-inch dice. Cut each slice of ham into 4 strips. Roll up each plumped prune in a strip of ham.

3 Thread the veal and prune and ham rolls on to 4 kebob skewers.

4 Heat the honey and wine vinegar in a small pan until the honey has dissolved. Season to taste. Brush the threaded kebobs first with oil and then with the honey baste.

5 Place the kebobs on the rack of a broiler pan. Cook under a preheated broiler for about 6 minutes on each side, brushing the kebobs with the honey baste halfway through cooking.

Serves 4

Preparation time: 20 minutes, plus standing overnight
Cooking time: 12 minutes

VEAL AND FONTINA CHEESE ROLLS

These veal rolls have a better flavor when cooked over the barbecue, but if this is impossible they can be cooked in a preheated oven at 375°F for about 15–20 minutes. The veal rolls and aioli can be made up to 24 hours in advance. Keep separate, cover, and chill.

¾ stick sweet butter, softened
2 tablespoons chopped fresh parsley
1 tablespoon chopped sage
1 garlic clove, minced
finely grated zest of 1 lemon
6 long thin veal escalopes, total weight about 1 pound
6 thin slices Parma ham
6 very thin slices Fontina or Mozzarella cheese, total weight about 6 ounces
4 tablespoons olive oil, for brushing
salt and pepper

Aioli di Marsala:
2 garlic cloves, minced
2 teaspoons Dijon mustard
1 teaspoon lemon juice
2 egg yolks
1 cup olive oil
2 tablespoons Marsala
salt and pepper

To garnish:
sage leaves
lemon slices

1 Mix the softened butter with the parsley, sage, garlic, lemon zest, and salt and pepper to taste.

2 Beat each escalope into a rectangle, measuring about 8 x 5 inches. Halve each escalope widthwise, and halve the slices of ham and cheese so that they are roughly the same size as the pieces of veal.

3 Spread each piece of veal with the flavored butter. Top with a slice of ham, then with a slice of cheese, and roll up tightly and neatly to enclose the ham and cheese. Tie securely with pieces of kitchen string.

4 Put the veal rolls into a shallow dish, cover, and chill for 8 hours.

5 To make the aioli, mix the garlic with the mustard, lemon juice, and salt and pepper to taste. Beat in the egg yolks and then beat in the olive oil, drop by drop. Finally, stir in the Marsala. (The aioli can be made in a food processor or blender, if preferred.) Spoon into a covered container and chill for 8 hours.

6 Take 4 kebob skewers and thread 3 veal rolls lengthwise on to each one. Brush all over with the olive oil.

7 Cook on the greased grill of a preheated barbecue for 8–10 minutes, turning the skewers once. Remove the veal rolls from the skewers and cut off the string.

8 Serve the veal rolls hot, garnished with sage leaves and lemon slices, with the Aioli di Marsala and a fennel salad.

Serves 6
Preparation time: 45 minutes, plus 8 hours chilling time
Cooking time: 8–10 minutes

BARBECUED BEEF SIRLOIN

To spit-roast, it is essential to have an indirect all-round heat, so push the coals on the barbecue away from the center to form a circle around the beef. Put a tray underneath the meat to catch the juices that drip (this also prevents any flare-ups) and use these juices to baste the meat.

I x 3–4-pound boneless sirloin of beef, rolled and tied
3 tablespoons olive oil
I tablespoon lemon juice
3 large onions, sliced
melted butter, for basting
I tablespoon all-purpose flour
salt and pepper

1 Rub the beef with the olive oil and sprinkle with the lemon juice. Place half the onion slices in a dish, put the beef on top and cover with the remaining onion. Leave to marinate for at least 3 hours.

2 Discard the onions. Insert the rotisserie spit into the beef and cook over hot coals with a drip pan placed directly beneath the spit to catch the meat juices (see recipe introduction). Baste frequently with melted butter.

3 After about 20 minutes, when the beef is well browned, dust it with the flour. Allow the flour to dry to a crust, then baste again. Cook the beef for a further 1¼ hours, basting from time to time, until the meat is tender and cooked to your liking. Season with salt and pepper.

4 To serve, remove the kitchen string and carve the beef into thin slices. Skim the fat from the juices in the drip pan and pour the juices over the beef.

Serves 8
Preparation time: 15 minutes, plus 3 hours marinating time
Cooking time: 1½–1¾ hours

PEPPERED STEAK FLAMED WITH BRANDY

4 filet mignon steaks, about 6 ounces each
1 tablespoon finely crushed
black peppercorns
¾ stick butter, melted
2 garlic cloves, minced
4 slices French bread, ½ inch thick, slightly
larger than the steaks
4 tablespoons brandy
salt

1 Press both sides of each filet mignon steak into the crushed peppercorns and season with salt.

2 Heat the butter with the garlic. Brush the steaks on both sides with the garlic butter.

3 Place the steaks on the greased grill of a preheated barbecue and cook for about 2½–3½ minutes. Turn the steaks over and cook for a further 2½–3½ minutes.

4 Just before the steaks are done to your liking, dip the French bread into the garlic butter, and toast quickly on both sides over the barbecue.

5 Place the toasted bread on 4 serving dishes and arrange a cooked steak on each slice.

6 Pour the brandy into a heatproof ladle or a small pan and heat over the barbecue. Carefully set the brandy alight and pour it, flaming, over the steaks. Serve as soon as the flames die down, accompanied by a simple green salad.

Serves 4
Preparation time: 8 minutes
Cooking time: 5–7 minutes (depending on how well you like your steak cooked)

MUSTARD STEAKS

4 filet mignon steaks, about 6 ounces each
4 tablespoons whole grain mustard
4 tablespoons soft light brown sugar
salt and pepper

1 Season the steaks with salt and pepper. Mix the mustard and sugar together and spread half the mixture over one side of each steak.

2 Place the steaks, mustard side up, on the oiled grill of a preheated barbecue and cook for 3–4 minutes. Turn over and spread with the remaining mustard mixture. Cook for a further 3–4 minutes, or until the steaks are cooked according to taste. Serve with plain baked potatoes

Serves 4
Preparation time: 5 minutes
Cooking time: 6–8 minutes

BEEF MEDALLIONS WITH MUSHROOM DUXELLES

1 tablespoon soya or corn oil
2 cups finely chopped open
cup mushrooms
2 shallots or small onions, finely chopped
¾ cup finely chopped walnuts
2 celery sticks
2 carrots
2 zucchini
1¼ cups beef broth
1¼ cups red wine
6 filet mignon steaks, about
4–5 ounces each
salt and pepper

1 First make the Mushroom Duxelles; heat the oil in a small saucepan and fry the mushrooms and shallots or small onions, stirring constantly, for about 5 minutes. Simmer, uncovered, until all the liquid has evaporated. Stir in the walnuts, with salt and pepper to taste. Keep warm.

2 Cut the celery, carrots, and zucchini into 1½-inch lengths. Cut them lengthwise into very fine julienne strips.

3 Put the beef broth in a pan and bring to the boil, then add the vegetable strips and boil for 3 minutes. Remove the strips with a slotted spoon and keep warm.

4 To make the sauce, boil the broth rapidly, uncovered, until reduced by about half. Add the red wine and season to taste with salt and pepper. Bring back to the boil for 1 minute, then set aside but keep hot.

5 Under a preheated hot broiler, cook the steaks for about 3–6 minutes on each side, or until they are cooked to your liking.

6 Serve the steaks on a bed of julienne vegetables with a spoonful of mushroom duxelles on each slice. Pour the sauce over carefully.

Serves 6
Preparation time: 20 minutes
Cooking time: 6–12 minutes

FILLET STEAK WITH SMOKED OYSTERS

6 filet mignon steaks, about
4–5 ounces each
2 tablespoons soya or corn oil
1 cup thinly sliced onions
2 cups thinly sliced button mushrooms
¼ cup red wine
¼ cup beef broth
3 tablespoons tomato paste
1 x 3½-ounce can smoked oysters, drained
salt and pepper
watercress sprigs, to garnish

1 Carefully cut three-quarters of the way through each steak and open out "butterfly fashion". Place the steaks between 2 sheets of waxed paper and beat them with a rolling pin to an even thickness. Sprinkle with salt and pepper and brush lightly with 1 tablespoon of oil.

2 Place under a preheated hot broiler and cook for 3–5 minutes each side, until they are cooked to your liking.

3 Meanwhile, heat the remaining oil in a pan and sauté the onions and mushrooms for a few minutes until they have softened. Add the wine, broth, and tomato paste and simmer for 3–4 minutes, until the liquid is slightly reduced and the sauce thickened. Stir in the drained oysters.

4 To serve, spoon the sauce over the steaks and garnish with sprigs of watercress.

Serves 6
Preparation time: 10 minutes
Cooking time: 6–10 minutes

BEEF KEBOBS WITH MARMALADE AND GINGER

I pound beef tenderloin
I large orange bell pepper, deseeded and
cut into 1-inch squares
¼ cup orange marmalade
2-inch piece fresh ginger root,
peeled and grated
I tablespoon soya or corn oil
sage leaves
orange strips, to garnish

I Trim any visible fat from the beef and cut it into 1-inch slices. Put the beef in a bowl with the bell pepper, marmalade, ginger, and oil and mix well to coat the pieces evenly.

2 Thread the beef on to 4 wooden skewers with bell pepper squares and sage leaves in between. Cook over the barbecue or under a preheated moderate broiler, turning the skewers frequently, for about 8 minutes, or until the beef is cooked to your liking. Serve garnished with orange strips.

Serves 4
Preparation time: 10 minutes
Cooking time: 8 minutes

STEAKS WITH SOY AND COCONUT

4 lean beef tenderloin steaks,
about 6 ounces each
½ cup soy sauce
½ cup medium dry sherry
2 tablespoons sesame or soya oil
2 tablespoons desiccated coconut,
toasted until golden
2 scallions, finely chopped

I Trim any visible fat from the steaks. Lay them in a wide dish and pour over the soy sauce, sherry, and oil. Cover the dish and place it in the refrigerator for 4 hours, or overnight.

2 Drain the steaks, reserving the marinade, and cook them over a hot barbecue or under a preheated broiler for 3–4 minutes on each side, until they are cooked to your liking, brushing frequently with the marinade.

3 Just before serving, sprinkle the steaks with toasted coconut and chopped scallions. Serve with a crisp salad.

Serves 4
Preparation time: 5 minutes, plus 4 hours marinating time
Cooking time: 6–8 minutes

MINCE AND MUSHROOM BURGERS

2 cups lean ground beef
1 small onion, finely chopped
1½ cups finely chopped
open cup mushrooms
2 cups fresh whole wheat bread crumbs
finely grated zest of ½ lemon
1 egg, beaten
2 tablespoons whole wheat flour
salt and pepper

To serve:
12 whole wheat buns, warmed
1 lettuce, shredded
4 firm tomatoes, sliced

1 In a bowl, mix together the beef, onion, mushrooms, and bread crumbs. Stir in the lemon zest and beaten egg to bind the mixture. Season lightly with salt and pepper.

2 Dust your hands with the flour and form the beef and mushroom mixture into 12 flat burgers.

3 Cook them over a barbecue, or under a preheated hot broiler, for 8–10 minutes, turning once, until they are lightly browned and cooked through.

4 To serve, split open the warm buns and place the burgers inside with shredded lettuce and sliced tomato.

Serves 6
Preparation time: 15 minutes
Cooking time: 8–10 minutes

GUINNESS-MARINATED STEAKS

Delicious for a barbecue, these steaks also make a perfect winter dinner party dish. After reducing the marinade, add a few tablespoons of heavy cream and heat quickly until thickened to make a sensational rich sauce.

4 beef tenderloin steaks,
about 8 ounces each
1 tablespoon olive oil
salt and pepper

Marinade:
2 teaspoons Dijon mustard
5 cloves
1½ tablespoons soft dark brown sugar
1 x 2-inch piece cinnamon stick, crumbled
6 black peppercorns, lightly crushed
1¼ cups Guinness

1 Trim all but a thin margin of fat off the steaks, then place them in a shallow dish.

2 Mix together the marinade ingredients and pour over the steaks. Cover and leave in a cool place for at least 6 hours, turning the steaks after 3 hours.

3 Five minutes before cooking the steaks, remove from the marinade and pat dry with paper towels.

4 Strain the marinade into a small heavy-based saucepan and boil rapidly until reduced by nearly half. This can be done either in the kitchen or on the barbecue itself.

5 Brush one side of each steak with a little olive oil and a little of the reduced marinade, then cook, oiled-side down, on a preheated greased barbecue grill over hot coals for 3–4 minutes for rare steaks; 4–5 minutes for medium; or 5–6 minutes for well done. Baste with a little more marinade while cooking.

6 Brush the steaks with oil, then turn over and cook for 3–6 minutes on the other side, again basting with the remaining marinade. Season generously with salt and pepper just before serving.

Serves 4
Preparation time: 10 minutes, plus 6 hours marinating time
Cooking time: 12–18 minutes

TERIYAKI MARINATED STEAK

4 tablespoons soy sauce
3 tablespoons dry sherry or sake
2 tablespoons oil
1 tablespoon lemon juice
1 tablespoon light brown sugar
1 tablespoon grated fresh ginger root
1 garlic clove, minced
4–6 steaks, 1-inch thick and weighing about 8 ounces, or 1–2 flank steaks, each about 1½ pounds
salt and pepper

1 Combine the soy sauce, sherry or sake, oil, lemon juice, sugar, ginger, garlic, and salt and pepper in a shallow dish in which the steaks will fit side by side.

2 Stir the ingredients together until well mixed, then add the steaks. Turn the steaks to coat both sides with the marinade, then cover the dish and marinate at cool room temperature, or in the refrigerator, for at least 4 hours. Turn the steaks over occasionally.

3 If the steaks have been marinated in the refrigerator, let them return to room temperature before cooking.

4 Grill the steaks 5–6 inches above hot coals, allowing about 5 minutes on each side for rare meat, and 7–8 minutes for medium. (Grill flank steak for 4–6 minutes on each side for rare to medium.) Baste occasionally with the marinade.

5 Transfer the steaks to a hot platter and serve. If using flank steak, cut diagonally into thin slices.

Serves 4–6
Preparation time: 10 minutes, plus 4 hours marinating time
Cooking time: 10–16 minutes

CLASSIC HAMBURGERS

The classic hamburger is incredibly simple to make; it consists of meat only.

I pound best quality ground lean beef
a little fat or oil, for frying
salt and pepper

To serve:
hamburger buns
tomato relish (see page 12)
lettuce leaves
cheese slices

I Season the ground beef with salt and pepper, and form into 6 round flat cakes. If the meat is very lean, you will need to grease the broiler pan, barbecue grill or skillet with a very little fat or oil. If there is a reasonable amount of fat in the meat, this is not necessary. The grill or skillet should be preheated so that the meat starts to cook the moment it touches the surface.

2 Grill the hamburger over a barbecue or under a hot broiler for 8–10 minutes, turning once. Alternatively, fry in a skillet.

3 Serve the burgers on toasted hamburger buns and with tomato relish, lettuce and cheese slices, if you wish.

Makes 6
Preparation time: 10 minutes
Cooking time: 4–6 minutes

INDEX